Four Proven Marketing Systems That Local Businesses Use to Fuel Growth and Outperform the Competition

How Businesses Focused on These Four Systems Dominate Their Market!

Table of Contents

Let's Ignite Growth In Your Business 1

   Main Driver #1: Search 5

   Main Driver #2: Social 9

   Main Driver #3: Mobile 15

Four Key Marketing Systems 21

   R1: Reputation 25

   R2: Reach 29

   R3: Resell 35

   R4: Referral 39

Assess Where You're At Right Now 45

   Is Your Business Being Left Behind? 51

What Are You Doing to Optimize the Four R's? 55

About the Author 59

(Psst! Write in this book!)
This is your copy, so feel free to highlight, underline, and take notes. You won't get in trouble—we promise!

Let's Ignite Growth In Your Business

What I'm about to show you can ignite growth in your business well beyond the levels you've likely achieved in the past.

Doesn't matter if you're a cosmetic surgeon, attorney, dentist, plumber, or any other type of local business that provides a needed service to your community.

How do I know this is true?

Because 95% of the clients I have worked with over the years are missing AT LEAST two out of the four critical, proven marketing systems that are necessary to achieve maximum business growth.

And the clients who are leveraging all four?

They're growing... *Fast!*

So unless your situation is completely out of the ordinary (which is possible but unlikely), **there is a really big opportunity to accelerate the growth of your business.**

And the acceleration I'm talking about isn't a short-lived "sugar-rush" kind of growth. It's the sustainable and responsible kind—the kind that complements your ethical standards and supports your long-term vision for your business.

Skeptical?

I understand. But as you continue reading, you'll discover that the systems I'm talking about aren't gimmicky, revolutionary or impossible to implement. They don't require you to turn your business model upside down or become something you're not.

Nor are they dependent on the latest new gizmo whatchamacallit that everyone and their brother wants to sell you.

In fact, **these four elements are the foundational building blocks that every successful business must optimize in order to achieve the growth they're looking for.**

But again, my experience tells me that most local businesses are not taking complete (or efficient) advantage of each of the four pieces we're about to go over.

Who am I?

My name is Jon Nare and I'm a sales, marketing, and operations strategist. Through a complimentary strategy session I work with a business owner to identify the biggest problems facing their business in the areas of getting new customers, getting referrals, and getting repeat business.

The outcome of this strategy session is a simple to implement action plan that automates getting more new customers, more referrals, and more repeat business.

The result is explosive revenue and profits, in some cases double or even triple in as little as 90 days.

At the end of the day, my job is to be an expert in marketing, and specifically local marketing that leverages technology to achieve maximum results, so that my clients can focus on what they do best:

Running their business, servicing their customers (clients, patients – we'll just go with customers to keep it simple) to the best of their ability, and keeping it profitable.

I've got a lot to share with you about how local businesses can dominate their market and take their income to entirely new levels, but of course we have limited time together so I am going to do my best to give you the high points over the course of this short book.

In the Last 10 Years, There Have Been Dramatic Changes in the Marketplace

The competitive landscape for local businesses has changed dramatically over the last several years, and will continue to change at an unprecedented pace.

Why? The continued development and distribution of technology has radically changed the way consumers are buying - how they hear about products and services; how they research them; and how they make a final purchase decision.

There are three main drivers of this change that are impacting your business. You need to be aware of them and you need to leverage them. Now let's run through each major driver.

Main Driver #1: Search

*According to Google, 97% of consumers search for **local** businesses online.*

First, a look at the numbers.

According to recent poll data from the Pew Internet and American Life Project, 92% of adult Internet users in the U.S. use a search engine (e.g. Google, Bing) to find information online - with the majority of this group performing keyword searches on a regular basis.

These statistics simply underline what you and I already know:

Search is King.

> *When you look at educated and affluent individuals, search engine use climbs to as high as 98%.*

Everyone who has access to the Internet uses a search engine to find relevant and useful information, and according to Google's own data, 97% of consumers search for **local** businesses online.

Got visibility?

The upshot of these facts is clear: If you want visibility for your business, you need visibility in the search engines, particularly Google.

Search isn't just king - it's a kingmaker too. High visibility in Google can mean more website traffic, more customers and referrals, more sales activity, and more profit for your local business.

And for those businesses in hyper-competitive markets, search-engine visibility can be the difference between being an unknown also-ran and being the Top Dog.

The good, the bad and the ugly: there for all to see

But visibility is a double-edged sword. Customer reviews of your business are visible too.

What if some of these reviews are negative?

What if they're *scathing*?

Well, the bad news is they can haunt your business for years and have a crushing impact on your bottom line and drive people to your competitors.

On the flip side, good reviews published all over the internet can fuel positive word of mouth and generate referral traffic like you've never seen!

Ranking matters

Here's what we know about how people use search engines: after entering a keyword into Google and being presented with pages and pages of blue text links, consumers generally don't dive very deeply into the results (95.91% of all clicks occur on page one).

And of page one results, people tend to focus on the top three. According to an Optify study, the top three positions for any given term account for nearly 60% (58.5) of the traffic. The top result alone commands an average click-through rate (CTR) of 36.4%.

So it's not enough to be "on Google." If you want to take advantage of the popularity of search, your website needs to be listed at the top of the page and above the "scroll line" for the search terms relevant to your business.

Now there are a number of ways to make your business more visible and gain the attention of your ideal type of customer. We'll talk about that in a bit.

But first, let's get into the next driver of change that's impacting your business today.

Main Driver #2: Social

Small businesses have (finally) embraced social media. According to HubSpot, 90% of small businesses are on Facebook, and 66% of them are spending more time on social media than they did a year ago.

We've all heard enough hype about social media to last a lifetime (or two). But there's a good reason, because there's actually something to the hype.

The social web has truly been a game changer.

Suddenly the norm

And the rapid rise of social media is pretty breathtaking.

> *Study: 59% of U.S. consumers use social media to vent about customer care frustrations.*

Just think: Facebook grew from a curiosity in a Harvard dormitory to a global force with over 1 billion users... in less than a decade.

Facebook seems like old news now - a presence in our lives that we take for granted. But it's worth remembering how recently this shift has taken place.

Not just for kids

A common misunderstanding that small businesses have is that Facebook and other networks are just for kids, and thus their target market isn't represented demographically on the site.

But the stats tell another story - the opposite story, in fact.

In the U.S., almost two-thirds of all Facebook users are over the age of 35. Recent Pew research reveals that **two-thirds** of U.S. adults use social networking sites like Facebook and Twitter.

High engagement

People aren't just ON social networks. They're GLUED to them.

The average U.S. Facebook user spends a whopping **7 hours and 46 minutes on the site each month**.

That's a full 15.5 minutes the average American spends on Facebook every single day!

The upshot of all of these numbers is pretty straightforward, but I'll spell it out just in case:

Your customers are on Facebook!

They spend a LOT of time there. They're sharing, tweeting, liking, pinning, friending, starring, following, fanning, posting, hash tagging, uploading, retweeting... you name it.

So if you want to reach them, capture their attention and make a pitch for your services before your competitors do... you've got to at least meet them halfway.

Sharing experiences... and frustrations

People are taking to the web to share their experiences with brands, and what they're sharing with their friends and family members isn't always flattering...

According to a current study from the Society for Communications Research, 59% of U.S. consumers are using social media to **vent** about customer care frustrations.

This isn't just happening on Facebook, but on sites like Angie's List, Yelp, Google+ Local and others. According to research from Deloitte & Touche, **7 in 10** who read reviews **share** them with friends, family and colleagues, amplifying the impact of these comments even further.

More and more local businesses are beginning to realize that, while they can't control what people say online, they can (and should) monitor and contribute to the conversation in an effort to influence the overall tenor.

They're realizing that having a **proactive online presence** that's focused on **adding value to the customer experience** is the surest way to grow and preserve their brand reputation… and protect themselves from the stray musings of a few unhappy souls.

Keeping pace with buyer expectations

Another big reason to get involved in social media is that you have to do it to **stay relevant**.

Your buyers expect it, and if you fall short of their expectations, they'll be more likely to spend their money with the guy down the street.

Even way back in 2008, a Cone Business study on social media found that **93% of customers expected companies to have a presence on social channels**, and **85% expected companies to interact with them on those social channels**.

That figure has only grown as the social media era has matured.

The perception out there is almost to the point where you're not considered a REAL business (worth trusting) if you're not on Facebook and keeping your business page updated on a regular basis.

You can either join the conversation or let your competitors do all the talking.

It's up to you!

Let's take a look at the third driver of change that you need to be aware of.

Main Driver #3: Mobile
("The really, really big one")

According to research from Mobile Marketer, 70% of all mobile searches result in action within one hour!

Look around you: You'll see a steady stream of consumers surfing the web on smartphones, iPads, Nooks, and Kindles.

And this is a trend that's hardly slowing.

It's almost impossible to overestimate the impact of the mobile computing revolution.

> *In their recent Mobile Internet Report, Morgan Stanley projects that mobile browsing will outpace desktop-based access within 3–5 years.*

In fact, the proliferation of cellphones, smartphones, e-readers and tablet PCs might be one of the most **underestimated** and **under-hyped** shifts in business today.

Today, 87% of Americans have mobile phones. It's their number one most-used technology device, with 73% saying so versus only 58% saying it's their desktop PC.

When you pause to consider what these newfangled devices are capable of, and how quickly they emerged from high-priced novelties to ever-present, "can't live without them"[1] gadgets... it's pretty unbelievable.

Marc Andreessen, co-creator of Netscape, the first widely used web browser, adds some helpful perspective: *"We have never lived in a time with the opportunity to put a computer in the pocket of 5 billion people. Practically everyone is going to have a*

---

[1] To illustrate this point, consider this statistic from Unisys: It takes 26 hours for the average person to report a lost wallet. It takes only 68 minutes for them to report a lost phone.

general purpose computer in their pocket, it's so easy to underestimate that, that has got to be **the really, really big one.***"*

A recent article in the Economist magazine adds this:

The potential of the smartphone age is deceptive. We look around and see more people talking on phones in more places and playing Draw Something when they're bored. This is just the beginning. In time, business models, infrastructure, legal environments, and social norms will evolve, and the world will become a very different and dramatically more productive place.

The revolution will be mobilized

It's clear that the future of the web is tied to smartphones and tablets and other mobile devices. More and more, people who visit your website will do so from a small-screened device instead of a hulking desktop or laptop.

What does that mean to you, the local business owner?

An Asymco study found that people have adopted mobile phone technology faster than almost any other household technology.

It means that if you want an effective web presence that supports your business goals, you need to have a website that supports a multitude of platforms, specifically the smartphone.

In fact, a study from Google found that that 6 in 10 mobile users will leave a website if it's not optimized for small screens.

If your businesses website looks cramped, cluttered, or illegible when viewed on a tablet or smartphone, you run the very real risk of turning away your most valuable asset: your customers.

In a weak economy, mobile matters

Think this "mobile" stuff is much ado about nothing? Let's put this into perspective…

The economic recovery is a sluggish one. People are still worrying about losing their jobs. Millions of homeowners owe more on their mortgage loans than what their homes are worth. Credit-card debt continues to weigh down U.S. households.

These are challenging times for consumers. As a local business, you don't want to give them any more reasons not to buy your services. Further, you don't want to add any additional friction to the process of buying your services!

A streamlined website for mobile is a new must-have. Particularly when you consider that people with smartphones are still turning to search engines to look for information.

Search to purchase

What's more, studies show that when people use their smartphones to search for information, they're more apt to take immediate action. They search from where they are and go immediately to what they find.

According to research from Mobile Marketer, 70% of all mobile searches result in action *within one hour!*

Answer This!

How does your website look and perform on a small screen? What kind of experience are you providing to would-be buyers?

[ ] Good user experience
[ ] So-so user experience
[ ] Poor user experience

Go ahead and pull out your phone. Open up your website. Can a visitor instantly call you with one click of a button? Can they instantly see a map that directs them to your office?

Four Key Marketing Systems

What all of this means to YOU!

Alright, raise your hand if any of these are true for you:

➤ Do you search online before deciding what businesses to buy from?

➤ Do you choose a service or product based on the recommendations you heard from friends over social media or reviews you've read?

➤ Do you carry a smartphone with you at all times?

Needless to say, these are true for many people!

And again, these trends are only accelerating.

As much as we might wish they'd go away and let us continue with business as usual the way it used to be…

the search/social/mobile paradigm is not going anywhere. It's here to stay.

The important thing now is to ask the hard questions and seek out the answers—even if they shake things up a bit:

➢ How do these changes impact the way consumers interact with my business?

➢ How do these changes impact the growth of my business?

➢ How do these changes impact the way I approach the marketing of my business?

Dramatic Change Calls For …
A Renewed Focus on the Fundamentals!

Given all of these revolutionary changes we've discussed - search, social and mobile - you might be worried that you are going to have to make drastic, revolutionary changes in your business.

That's not necessarily the case.

Our experience shows that **there are four key marketing systems that need to be optimized in order to** *maximize growth* in today's wired, always-on and hyper-competitive marketplace.

The marketing systems we're about to present aren't even new!

They're not hifalutin' gimmicks that were cooked up in the ivory tower or by some pie-in-the-sky TED-talk guru.

They're proven concepts that have been tested, re-tested and tested again in the marketplace for as long as business has been conducted.

Now, sure, some of the tactics and mediums have changed, but the strategies themselves haven't.

As it happens, these four essential areas all start with the letter "R."

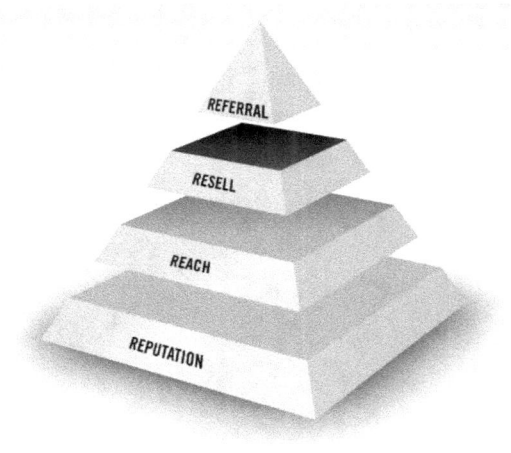

➢ Reputation

➢ Reach

➢ Resell

➢ Referral

These are the four things *every* local business needs to plan for and optimize to maximize their growth potential.

Data shows, and my experience proves, that **each of these can account for about 25% growth on their own, and combined have a compounding effect that can ignite growth to 100% or more**.

Let's briefly run through each element and explore how maximizing these 4 R's could significantly impact growth in your business.

R1: Reputation

What are you doing to proactively manage, protect and monetize your most valuable asset—your reputation?

The first R is **Reputation**. This can also be considered your brand or how you're seen in your local marketplace.

As we discussed earlier, it has never been easier for potential customers to find out what others think about your business. This is both good and bad (depending on what people find).

As you know, nowadays people search online before they buy. We know that people put a lot of stock in what they find and read online. In fact, a recent Nielsen study shows that 74% of U.S. consumers choose to do business based on online feedback - even when it's feedback from total strangers!

According to Nielsen's summary of their poll data, recommendations from personal acquaintances and opinions posted by consumers online are "the most trusted forms of advertising."

Look who's talking (about <u>you</u>)…

- ➢ Customers
- ➢ Potential Customers
- ➢ Competitors
- ➢ Disgruntled employees
- ➢ Ex-spouses
- ➢ Former business partners, investors
- ➢ Trolls (the permanently aggrieved)

This probably isn't anything new to you, and there's a decent chance that, like most of the owners I talk to, you are not very pleased about some of the things people have written about your business!

This brings up a larger point.

Whether it is positive or negative in tone, **most of the content about your business that is available online is not even being created by you anymore!**

Consumers are critics and publishers now. They all carry tiny "printing presses" in their pockets (remember those mobile devices)!

Study: 90% of consumers online trust recommendations from people they know; 70% opinions of unknown users.

Reputation: more important than ever

There's no denying, local businesses have always relied on their reputation.

But the stakes are even higher today because of how easy it is for consumers to find information about local businesses before they buy.

What's more, as we've already discussed, negative reviews can get lodged in the search results, hanging like an albatross around your neck and dragging down sales.

In today's world, the first thing most people do when they hear about your business (whether from an ad you paid for or a referral from a friend) is look you up online.

The question is what do they see when they Google your name or the name of your business?

Do they see websites with info about your business? Is this info accurate (current address, phone, etc)? Do they see good or bad reviews (no reviews is not much better than bad reviews)?

Obviously, having a positive footprint online that helps build trust in those who are looking to hire you to solve their problem is key to generating more sales.

Answer This!

Are you "Googleable"? How many pages of Google are you on? (You may include Search, Maps, and Google+ Local citations in your answer)

[ ] Don't know
[ ] 0
[ ] 1
[ ] 2–5
[ ] 6+

R2: Reach

What are you doing to ensure that more people know about you today than yesterday?

The second R is **Reach**. It's my experience that *a local business that wants to grow needs to make sure that more people know about it today than did yesterday*.

If you're not meeting new people and telling them about your services, you're not developing a pipeline of potential new customers and you are going to see fewer sales in the future as a result.

This sounds pretty obvious, I know. But I'm always surprised when I talk to local business owners and ask them about their promotional efforts.

When I look at the pipeline-filling activities of local businesses, I see mostly a scattershot approach.

A campaign here and there… with only a vague idea on whether they are getting a positive return on their investment.

No wonder so many local businesses become skeptical of marketing:

They're doing it all wrong!

Very rarely do I see coordinated, systematic and metrics-driven efforts to reach a wider audience and drive more prospects (i.e. people who are interested in what you're selling) through the front door.

But this kind of focused, ongoing and intentional approach is exactly what's necessary to reach more qualified prospects in a cost-effective - not to mention satisfying manner!

A once-in-awhile, ad hoc marketing strategy is not going to get the results you need to achieve consistent business growth.

Game Changing Advice

Let me share a little story from Todd Brown, an expert marketer and creator of the "Marketing Funnel Automation" system:

A few years ago I moved my family down to South Florida. I was tired of the cold New Jersey winters.

And I was ready for some palm trees and year-round gorgeous weather. A couple months after moving I became friends with Rich Schefren (the Founder of Strategic Profits). I later ran the marketing for Strategic Profits for a handful of years.

Well, very early before I was a partner at Strategic Profits, I had a meeting with Rich at a Starbucks café in Barnes and Noble in Boca Raton to talk about some of the struggles I was having growing my main company at the time.

And, it was at that meeting that Rich shared with me one single piece of advice that forever changed my business and income. To say it's been a game-changer is really an understatement.

Here's the gist of what he said:

"Until you can pay for the acquisition of customers, you do not have a real business. All you have is a promotion."

What Rich was saying was this... Until you are using paid traffic (media buying) to acquire new customers, you will continue to have ups and downs in lead flow, ups and downs in sales, ups and downs in income, and limited scalability (growth potential).

You see... reliance on social media, search engine optimization, and strategic partnerships makes your business vulnerable.

Vulnerable because... SEO algorithms change, partners flake out. And you have little if any REAL control. Whereas, once you understand even the basics of media buying... paid traffic... (both offline and online) **the game immediately changes for you.**

With paid traffic you have full control over what happens, when, where and how with your website traffic.

Your lead flow becomes steady, sales become consistent, and your income becomes dependable (assuming you have a good offer, of course). Fact is: with media buying done correctly, getting traffic to your site is never, ever a problem."

- Courtesy of Todd Brown, Marketing Funnel Automation

Now as a business owner myself, this was extremely eye opening. It changed not only how I run my business, but also how I help my own clients.

There is no shortage of marketing channels that can be used to get the word out about your business and the services you offer. And it's far better to have a multi-channel strategy in place than just a single channel strategy.

However, at the core should lay a solid steady stream of new customers that can only come from paid traffic. Imagine having the power of putting your message in front of the most targeted people who are most likely to hire you. Paid traffic enables you to do just that and combined with a tested sales funnel that both qualifies and pre-sells your services… BAM!

You just found Willy Wonka's golden ticket.

If you remember the story of Willy Wonka and the Chocolate Factory, only a select few received Willy Wonka's golden ticket, giving them access to a whole new world unseen by the rest of the world.

What you do with this knowledge is in your hands.

Many will end up sticking this book on a shelf somewhere and never take the action their business so desperately needs. Do not let that be you. Yes, all of this can be overwhelming… seek help from a professional today.

It's time to implement your own coordinated, systematic and metrics-driven marketing strategy that on a daily basis reaches out to your targeted audience and delivers them to you ready to buy.

Answer This!

Do you have a method to build a continually growing prospect/client email list?

[ ] Yes
[ ] No
[ ] We don't have a list

R3: Resell

> *What are you doing to upsell, cross sell and repeat sell to maximize the lifetime value of your customer base?*

The third R is **Resell**. Once you've done all of the hard and often costly work of getting a customer, you need to make sure to maximize the lifetime value, or LTV, of that customer.

Whatever metaphor you want to use... mining your backyard... picking the low hanging fruit... the point is the same:

It makes more sense (both financially and from an efficiency standpoint) to fully capitalize on your existing customer base than to be constantly on the hunt for new customers.

The more value you can generate from each customer, the less you have to spend on marketing, which means you can increase your profit margins and/or reinvest the savings into your services - in the process making your business even more attractive to your customers!

In practice, this can mean increasing the dollar value of each transaction or increasing the frequency that customers buy, either by offering add-on services or upsells or cross-sells.

McDonald's offers the classic example: 'Do you want fries with that?' or 'Do you want to supersize your order?'

These days there are so many cost effective and trackable ways to bring customers back to your business.

To give you just one quick example, consider an intelligent automated email campaign that goes out to every customer you work with.

A simple email is automatically sent out thanking them for choosing to work with you. This may be something you do right now.

Also in the email is a small section introducing them to other services your business provides.

Now remember, at this point, the customer loves you and your business (if you've done your job right). If they have need of anything else, you are at the top of their list before any other business.

Pay attention... here's the magic. Not only do you list your other services, but each service has its own link to a web page (or even a video) that explains more about that service. So where's the magic?

Each link is a trackable link that not only tells you what service(s) they have interest in, but also automatically adds them to a new list for that service they just showed interest in (all by clicking the link).

Not only can you now follow up with them by phone about this other service, they will also automatically receive a series of emails all about how you can help with this new service they have shown to have interest in.

Can you see the power in an automated system that you only have to take the time to set up once and will then consistently on autopilot, open the door and pre-sell customers on additional services?

All by simply adding customer email addresses to it.

Despite having easy access to the newest and coolest tools, most local businesses in your area are leaving money on the table because they're not maximizing the resell potential of each customer.

Answer This!

Do you ethically (but effectively) prepare buyers from their very first purchasing experience with you to keep coming back to purchase over and over again?

[ ] No
[ ] Yes
[ ] Not sure

R4: Referral

> *What are you doing to use your successful relationships to create new, organic opportunities so that you can spend less and make more?*

The fourth R is **Referral**.

Since you're doing such a great job taking care of your customers and keeping them happy, the next best thing you can do is set up systems to maximize the benefit you get from them, right? So that they are doing the marketing for you!

Well, it's well known that *if you just leave it up to people to do referrals for you, very few will - even if they are very happy with you*.

You have to make it very easy - almost effortless - for your happy customers to refer your business if you really want to maximize the referrals you generate from them.

A study from Lee Resource Inc. found that attracting a new customer can cost five times as much as keeping an existing one.

Referrals make great customers

We all want referrals because they help us save money on marketing, right?

Well, there's even more to gain from referrals than cost savings:

According to a case study noted in the Harvard Business Review, customers that come from referrals are, on average, about 18% more likely than others to stay with a company and they generate 16% more in profits!

And according to several case studies reported on by the website TechCrunch:

Friends referred by friends make better customers.

They spend more (a 2x higher estimated lifetime value than customers from all other channels at One Kings Lane); **convert better** (75% higher conversion than renters from other marketing channels at Rent the Runway); and **shop faster** (they make their first purchase after joining twice as quickly than referrals from other channels at Trendyol).

Why are referrals so powerful?

Because they channel the power of **social proof**. Social proof is a fancy way of saying that we humans are easily influenced by each other.

We're pack animals.

When a member of our pack (family) or tribe (social circle) recommends a product or service, we take that recommendation very seriously.

Similarly, when someone in a position of power, prestige or authority recommends something, we are very **quick to act** on that recommendation.

You see the applied power of social proof everywhere: in TV ads, when you see a celebrity endorsing a product; on the radio, when the person hosting the pledge drive tells listeners that so-and-so donated $50 to NPR; on the back of a novel you're reading, when you see testimonials from other notable authors; and on the web, when you visit sites like Yelp.com to read consumer reviews of local restaurants.

Moving from passive to active, ad hoc to systematic

Almost without fail, *most businesses I talk to have no clear referral generation system*.

They essentially think that referrals are something that you simply wait and hope for... but *the reality is that referrals don't just happen, you have to go out and get them!*

And if you're going to spend the time collecting them, you need a system that effectively channels your efforts into tangible results.

Amplify the power of referrals

It's not a secret that referrals are powerful and having a steady stream of them can really add to the bottom line of any local business.

The problem is they can be somewhat limiting as they typically travel from one person to the next one at a time.

Imagine having a process in place where word of mouth traveled one to many and instead of taking place in small private conversations, it was public and affected multiple people at a time.

You might be thinking social media and that can certainly play a part.

However, this power comes from getting happy clients to post good reviews about your business online (in places like Google, Yelp, Angie's List, etc.) and then marketing those positive reviews everywhere... on your website, on Facebook, on YouTube, etc.

This actually feeds right back into the first R... Reputation. If you remember from that section, a Nielsen study showed that 74% of U.S. consumers choose to do business based on online feedback - even when it's feedback from total strangers!

That means, reviews about your business published on various websites essentially have the power to act as a referral source because most people trust reviews from strangers in much the way they trust a recommendation from a friend.

No matter how you look at it, there's no denying the need for having a systemized process in place for generating a steady stream of new referrals.

Answer This!

How many formal, written referral-generating systems do you currently have with prospects or potential partners? (Check one)

[ ] 0
[ ] 1
[ ] 2–5
[ ] 6+

Assess Where You Are At Right Now

What parts are you missing?

Now, the problem is that most local businesses are operating without even being aware of these changes or marketing systems, and how it is impacting them.

Let me show you some examples ...

Failure to address issues

First, if you aren't effectively and proactively managing your reputation, you aren't aware of comments like this being made about your business:

Julie Miller
2 months ago

★ ☆ ☆ ☆ ☆   AWFUL!! Have never been so disrespected. I was injured in had the nerve to yell at me when I was admitted to a hospital for unrelated

Ouch. That hurts. Comments like these will negatively impact how others view your business in the marketplace. According to Nielsen, user reviews are "the most trusted form of advertising."

Imagine having an automatic feedback loop in place – allowing you to address issues before they are made public and getting positive reviews published all over the web helping to build trust and credibility in your marketplace.

Everyone else is mobile… except you
You have people looking for your business on their mobile phones, and your website is showing up like this:

You decide as you look at the image shown. Is that a good user experience?

No one wants to zoom in and out or scroll around trying to navigate this web page.

A study from Google found that 60% of users will leave a website if it's not optimized for mobile (small screens).

That's means over half of the people you're currently driving to your website are leaving (talk about lost money… especially if you're paying for ads).

While your competitors' mobile website is showing up like this:

People will stay on your competitor's website if it's properly optimized for a small touchscreen.

Not to mention Google gives preference to websites that are optimized for both desktop and mobile.

They are also more likely to call or visit with "Click-to-call" and GPS mapping technology.

Which local business do you think a potential customer would be more likely to visit just based on these two images?

Bleeding potential sales

Perhaps you have a great website that's driving calls on a daily basis from all of the wonderful marketing you're already doing.

Did you know that a good 95% of those people are leaving without taking any action simply because they're not ready to buy today?

With the right capture mechanism in place, you could be capturing 100% of those people and then marketing to them wherever they go on the internet for pennies on the dollar.

This allows you to stay in front of them until they are ready to make that all important buying decision.

Lost customers
Maybe you've been serving your community for some time now and have many happy customers you've served for a number of years.

Problem is you never got around to staying in contact with them regularly and now you have a big list of old customers who no longer buy from you for whatever reason.

Not only can you have an automated system for staying in front of current customers, you can also implement a customer reactivation campaign that will allow you to bring those lost customers back.

Since past customers are much more likely to buy from you, this campaign repeatedly delivers a huge return on investment over driving new customers.

So, how can we address some of these things?

Let me share some ideas... I obviously can't give you all of them in the space of this small book, but let me share a few worth pursuing:

➢ Control your own reviews with your own feedback site – allowing you to address issues before they are made public.

➢ Create a separate mobile site for your business that is optimized for mobile.

➢ Capture and follow up with people interested in what you do, but just are not ready to buy today.

➢ Keep in touch with people who have used your services. Integrate tools to help automate this.

➢ Reach more people more cost-effectively and with greater targeting using Google, Facebook, and YouTube ads.

➢ Ask for referrals when you first meet a potential customer and after you've delivered on your service.

Just one small shift in each of the four R's we've discussed can start to produce dramatic results.

Is Your Business Being Left Behind?

Now, if you fall into the category of local businesses that are not proactively working with these technology changes and marketing systems, **<u>you are only going to see things get worse over time</u>**.

These changes, though recent, are now a permanent part of the competitive landscape.

The gap between the local businesses that "get it" and those that don't is widening at an accelerating pace.

You can look at any industry and see examples of the handful of businesses that are really pulling away from the pack, and those that are falling behind.

It's time to go 'all-in'

Do you have someone that is helping your business in these areas?

Or are you kidding yourself into thinking that you are going to try to do this by yourself or with the very part-time effort of one of your employees that has no marketing background?

That's not going to cut it!

Do you watch "Parks and Recreation"? To paraphrase the wise Ron Swanson, **you can't half-ass two things. You've got to whole-ass one thing.**

If you're struggling to fit everything into your calendar already (most owners I talk to are), you're probably not going to have the bandwidth to optimize the four R's.

Either something else has to give, or you need to enlist a friendly expert to help you!

Answer the call

Get this: according to data from Google, **61% of local searches on a mobile phone result in a phone call**.

Are you ready, both literally and figuratively, to answer that call?

Or are you going to let it ring until one of your competitors picks up the phone?

> *Are you ready to answer the call? Or are you going to let it ring until one of your competitors picks up the phone?*

If you're ready to make a shift …

You may realize that you need to make a change, that you aren't growing like you should, that your current approach to marketing is not working, and that you are committed to getting past your current income limits.

If so, I would be interested in talking with you to see if there is potentially a good fit to work together.

However, I must say upfront that I only work with one client in your industry per city so I can give them all of my knowledge and experience without having to worry about conflict with another client.

And we are particular about who we work with.

We work with businesses that are already successful and are looking for strategic ways to get FAR MORE successful.

We work with clients that have the mindset and resources to handle the level of growth that is possible to achieve.

What to do next

If you've seen the benefit of what you've read in these pages and you decide you'd like some assistance so you can focus on running your business instead of all the tasks involved in marketing it, let me know.

We can take a close look at how your business is doing now, what's needed to improve your visibility, and how we can reach your goals together.

Reach out to me today

Jon Nare
True Inspired Solutions
Email: Jon@TrueInspiredSolutions.com
Phone: 480-331-8783
Web: TrueInspiredSolutions.com

I look forward to hearing from you!

What Are You Doing to Optimize the Four R's?

Reputation: *What are you doing to proactively manage, protect and monetize your most valuable asset—your reputation?*

_____

_____

_____

_____

_____

_____

_____

_____

_____

_____

Reach: *What are you doing to ensure that more people know about you today than yesterday?*

_____

_____

_____

_____

_____

_____

_____

_____

_____

_____

_____

_____

_____

_____

Resell: *What are you doing to upsell, cross sell and repeat sell to maximize the lifetime value of your customer base?*

_____

_____

_____

_____

_____

_____

_____

_____

_____

_____

_____

_____

_____

Referral: *What are you doing to use your successful relationships to create new, organic opportunities so that you can spend less and make more?*

_____

_____

_____

_____

_____

_____

_____

_____

_____

_____

_____

_____

About the Author

Jon Nare is a founding partner in True Inspired Solutions where he helps local business owners identify the biggest problems facing their business in the areas of getting new customers, getting referrals, and getting repeat business.

He then helps implement an action plan that automates getting more new customers, more referrals, and more repeat business.

The result is explosive revenue and profits, in some cases double or even triple in as little as 90 days.

When not helping local businesses, he can be found spending quality time with his loving wife, four children, and two grandchildren.

More details about Jon Nare can be found by going to his LinkedIn profile at:
>> TrueInspiredSolutions.com/linkedin/